Contents

Contents

Contents

Vocabulary

Learning New Words

Sometimes when you are reading you find words that are new to you. Here are some tips to help you learn new words.

Before You Read

TIP Look for **highlighted** words. These words are important to understanding the lesson. Here is an example from Lesson 1.

We find clues about how these people lived by looking at the **artifacts** they left behind.

TIP **Look at the new word.**
- Are there parts of the word you already know?
- Have you seen this word before?

While You Read

TIP **Look at the words around the new word.**
- The other words in a sentence can help you decide the meaning of a new word.

TIP **Write down the new word.**
- Write the new word in your Word Journal.
- Use resources such as your teacher or a dictionary to help you learn the meaning of the new word.
- Write the meaning of the word in your Word Journal.

After You Read

TIP **Use the word**
- Write your own sentence using the new word.
- Share your new words with your friends and family.
- Try to make a sentence that uses several of the new words you have learned.

Geography

It is thought that Native Americans were the first people to settle the land we now call the United States. Over the years, Native American groups settled in all regions of the country. They adapted to the land and climate of the region in which they settled. For example, parts of the Southwest region are hot and dry most of the year. Some groups in this region built homes made of dried clay. These homes stayed warm in the winter and cool in the summer.

Native Americans used the resources found in their region. These resources included forests, water, plants, and animals. In the Southeast and Northeast, Native Americans settled near rivers and used the water for farming. They hunted animals that lived in the forests.

Native American groups still live throughout the United States today. Many observe the same traditions and celebrations their group practiced long ago.

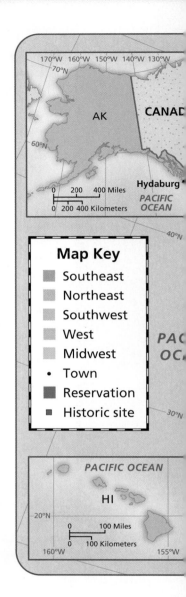

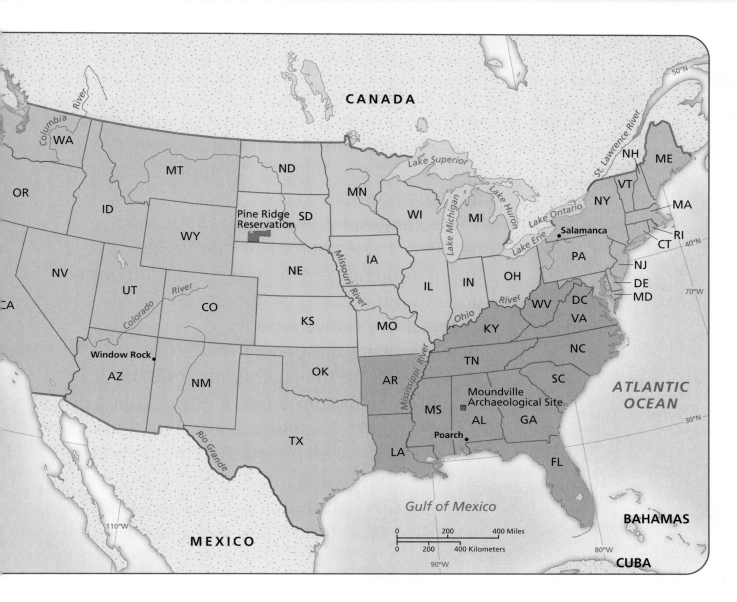

This map shows the regions of the United States. In this book, you will be reading about Native American groups from each region.

Early Native Americans

▲ This little toad was carved by Native Americans who lived thousands of years ago.

▼ Some early Native Americans lived in mountain regions.

In this book you will learn about many different groups of Native Americans. These groups are different from one another, but they all had one thing in common. Geography affected how they lived.

The **geography** of a region is the land features and resources of that region. Understanding geography will help you better understand why the land is especially important to Native Americans.

Geographers are people who study geography. One thing geographers study is landforms. Landforms are special shapes or forms on Earth's surface, such as mountains or flat areas called plains. Geographers also study natural resources. Natural resources are things in nature that people use, such as water or timber from trees. Geographers also study climate. **Climate** is the kind of weather a place has over time. Landforms, natural resources, and climate all shaped how Native Americans lived long ago.

In this book you will read about Native American groups and the different landforms of the places where they lived. You will find out how they used the natural resources around them. You will learn about how they made houses and clothing that fit the climate where they lived.

In this unit you will read about the Mississippian (miss uh SIP ee uhn) people. They lived in what is now the southeastern United States. The Mississippians lived on flat lands near streams that flow into the Mississippi River. They used the natural resource of rich land to grow many crops, such as corn and beans. The warm and rainy climate helped their crops to grow.

Keep reading to find out more about the lives of early Native Americans.

▼ Some early Native Americans lived on the plains or in the desert.

REVIEW How did geography affect the way the Mississippian people lived? **Main Idea and Details**

History of Early Native Americans

History tells the story of people and places in the past. In this book, you will read about Native American life long ago. You will also read about how Native Americans live today.

The ancestors of Native Americans were the first people to reach North America. Many scientists think they came to North America from Asia. But how did they get here?

Thousands of years ago, Earth went through long cold periods called Ice Ages. Huge sheets of ice covered much of North America. So much water was frozen into ice that ocean levels fell. The water level dropped so far that land appeared between Asia and North America. We call this land a "land bridge," because it was like a bridge people could walk across.

▲ The earliest people in North America made stone spearheads like the one above.

▼ With spearheads attached to long poles, people were able to hunt large animals such as mastodons.

4

Hunters may have followed animals across the land bridge from Asia to North America. Other people may have come by boat. When the Ice Ages ended, oceans rose and covered the land bridge.

Over thousands of years, people spread across North and South America. As groups settled in different places, they developed different ways of life. Land, natural resources, and climate in the places where these people settled affected how they lived.

We find clues about how people lived by looking at the artifacts they left behind. An **artifact** is an object made by people. Artifacts made by people long ago include tools, weapons, and pottery.

The Mississippian people left many artifacts. Old tools give us clues about how they worked. Artwork and masks tell us about their religion. By studying thousands of artifacts, scientists have developed a picture of Native American history.

REVIEW How might people first have come to North America?
Summarize

▲ **This Mississippian cup was used in ceremonies.**

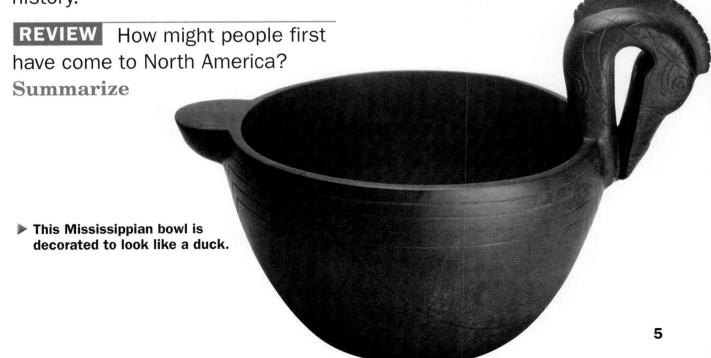

▶ **This Mississippian bowl is decorated to look like a duck.**

5

▲ Some early Native Americans gathered berries, nuts, and greens in the wild.

Economy of Early Native Americans

Everyone needs food, shelter, and clothing. The **economy** of a group of people is the way in which the people meet these needs. The economy includes the kind of work people do to get food, clothing, and shelter.

The first people to come to North America got their food by hunting and gathering. Men made spears by tying sharpened rocks to sticks. They hunted big animals such as woolly mammoths and bears. Women gathered plants and berries. All year long, groups moved from place to place and searched for food. They found shelter in caves. They may have made animal-skin tents. They also made clothes out of animal skins.

▼ Once people learned to farm, more people could live together.

Over time, many groups learned to farm. They planted crops such as corn, beans, squash, and pumpkins. They no longer depended only on hunting and gathering for food. They stopped moving from place to place. They built villages to live in.

Early Native Americans made most of the things they needed. They traded with other groups for things they could not make and for natural resources they could not get nearby. Trade was an important part of the economy of many early peoples. Living near rivers made trade easier.

The Mississippian people lived mostly by farming. They also did some hunting and gathering. Many artifacts left by the Mississippian people came from places that were far away. These artifacts show that the Mississippian people must have traded over long distances.

▼ Many groups traded food for seashells to make jewelry and other objects.

REVIEW How did early Native Americans get what they needed to survive? **Main Idea and Details**

68554

Government of Early Native Americans

Government is the way a group is run or ruled. Many Native American groups chose leaders to help them make important rules and decisions. When we study government, one of the things we study is the way that a group chooses its leaders.

The first people to come to North America may have lived in small bands, or groups of one or two families. In such a small group, everyone might join in making decisions. Some bands may have had leaders that had the final say.

Later on, when people began farming, they settled in villages. These larger groups depended on their leaders to make more of the group decisions.

A large village was built by a Mississippian people in what is now Alabama. We call it Moundville. About 1,000 people lived there. Many smaller villages surrounded Moundville. Moundville seems to have been a government center. People from nearby villages may have come there for important meetings and religious ceremonies.

▼ The leaders of most Native American groups gathered to make important decisions.

We call the town Moundville because it is filled with mounds, or huge piles of earth. The Mississippian people built these mounds. People studying this region think that leaders lived in houses on top of some mounds. Other mounds held religious temples, and some mounds were used to bury important people after they died.

Some mounds still exist today. Some of them are huge. It took many people many years to build them. Mississippian leaders and other important people probably directed the mound building. These leaders probably made other important decisions as well. They may have decided when to plant and harvest crops and when to hold festivals.

▲ Today Moundville is a park where people can learn about the Mississippian people.

REVIEW Why would Mississippian people need a government in order to build mounds? **Draw Conclusions**

FACT FILE

More Mounds

Many different Native American groups built mounds. The Great Serpent Mound in Ohio was built by the Adena people. It is shaped like a snake. The mound is about 1/4 mile long and 3 feet tall. Many students take field trips to see this amazing mound.

The Great Serpent Mound

Culture of Early Native Americans

Culture is the way of life shared by a group of people. Culture includes ideas, customs, and beliefs. Culture also includes the tools and weapons people use, and their government, economy, religion, and language.

One way we learn about cultures of long ago is by studying artifacts. For example, you have read that the Mississippian people were mound builders. The huge mounds were built over many years, one basketful of earth at a time. It took a lot of effort to build them. Some of the mounds were burial mounds. What does this tell us about Mississippian culture? It tells us that death and burial were very important to them.

The remains of houses also give us clues about a long-ago culture. Important Mississippian people lived in larger, fancier houses. Ordinary people lived in smaller, simpler houses.

▲ This carved seashell shows a bear and an eagle.

▼ This cover for a bottle was made to look like an opossum, a common animal in the southeastern United States.

10

Because of that we know that Mississippian culture included people of different social classes.

Some artifacts have pictures or designs on them. The images tell us what people liked and what was important to them. Sometimes there are religious symbols. Some artifacts represent people. Many Mississippian artifacts are decorated with birds and animals that were important to them.

It is important to remember that different Native American groups had different cultures. Some people think that all Native Americans were pretty much the same. This is not true. We know that there were hundreds of different Native American cultures. As you read this book, you will learn about some of them.

▲ This head was carved from a shell around 1,000 years ago.

REVIEW What is culture?
Main Idea and Details

▶ Some artifacts, like this pot, represent people.

Map and Globe Skills

Understand Map Grids

What? A **map grid** is a set of lines on a map. The lines cross each other. Many maps have grids. They can be found on maps of cities, states, and countries. There is even a map grid that is used on globes.

On maps with grids, there are letters and numbers along the edges. These are an important part of the map grid.

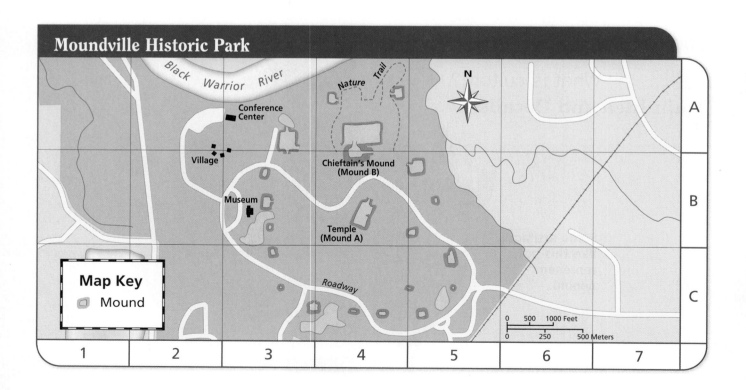

Moundville Historic Park

Black Warrior River

Nature Trail

N

Conference Center

Village

Chieftain's Mound
(Mound B)

Museum

Temple
(Mound A)

Map Key

Mound

Roadway

0   500   1000 Feet
0   250   500 Meters

A   B   C

1   2   3   4   5   6   7

Why? Mapmakers use grids to help people find places on maps. It is easy to follow the grid lines to the location you are looking for. You can use the grid on this map of Moundville to find the nature trail, the village, or any other place you want to locate. Because this is a small map, you might think grid lines are not important. Think about a really big map. The grid lines on this small map can help you learn how to read larger maps.

How? A grid is made of two sets of lines. One set of lines goes east and west. The other set of lines goes north and south. These two sets of lines cross each other. They make squares.

Look at the map of Moundville. Find the Temple (Mound A) and put your finger on it. Move your finger straight across to the right edge of the map. You come to the letter **B.**

Now put your finger back on the Temple. This time slide your finger straight down to the bottom edge of the map. You come to the number **4.** Now you know that the Temple is located in square B-4.

Think and Apply

1 What is the system of lines on this map called?

2 What is found in square A-3?

3 In which square is the museum located?

1. What is **geography**?

2. How did the land bridge between Asia and North America form?

3. What kinds of artifacts were left by early Native Americans?

4. Why would Native Americans who farmed live in a village, instead of moving from place to place?

5. Why would groups of Native Americans trade with each other?

6. What can we learn about the Mississippian culture from studying the mounds they built?

7. **Use a Map Grid** Draw a map of your classroom. Add lines, letters, and numbers to make a grid. Identify in which squares you would find your desk and the teacher's desk.

Link to ⟨⟩ **Writing**

Write a Report: Suppose you are a scientist writing about artifacts left by early Native Americans. Choose one artifact pictured in this unit and explain what it tells you about the people who made it.

Test Talk

Locate Key Words in the Question.

Directions: Finding key words can help you understand a question. Follow these steps.

- Read the question.
- Look for and circle key words in the question.
- Turn the question into a statement: "I need to find out _____ ."

Try It Read each question. Circle key words in each question. Then complete each sentence.

1. How many people lived in the Mississippian village of Moundville?
   - **A.** 10
   - **B.** 100
   - **C.** 1,000
   - **D.** 10,000

   I need to find out _____ .

2. What kind of economy did the Mississippian people have? Use details from the text to support your answer.

   I need to find out _____ .

These projects will help you learn more about early Native Americans.

The Anasazi

Write a report. The Anasazi were another early Native American group. The Anasazi lived more than 1,000 years ago in the Southwest region of the United States. One interesting fact about the Anasazi is that they often built their homes into the sides of cliffs and were sometimes called Cliff Dwellers. Use the Internet or an encyclopedia to find out more about the Anasazi. Write a short report telling what you have learned about the Anasazi. Draw a picture to go with your report. Put your report in a class book.

Visit the Mound Builders

Use a computer. Have an adult help you use the Internet to learn about visiting Native American mounds. You might choose to learn about visiting Moundville, the Great Serpent Mound, or another important mound location called Cahokia (ka HOH kee ah). Choose one. Take notes about the things you can see there. Give a short speech to the class about what your classmates would see on a field trip or vacation there.

▲ For the Iroquois, the turtle represented North America. The tree carved on this statue is the Tree of Peace. The eagle on the tree was a symbol of protection.

The Iroquois

Hi! My name is Jenny. I am a member of the Seneca Indian Nation. The Seneca (SEN i cuh) are one of the Six Nations that make up the Iroquois. I live with my family in the town of Salamanca (sah lah MAHN cah), New York. My town is on the Allegany Indian Reservation in western New York State. The Allegheny River flows through our reservation.

The climate here is cold in the winter with short, warm summers. During the winter, snow and ice cover the ground.

Long ago, forests covered much of the Iroquois lands. My ancestors gathered berries and nuts in the forest. An **ancestor** is a relative who lived long ago. They used wood from the forest to make homes and tools.

They hunted deer, beaver, and moose. The animals were used for food and their skins were used to make clothing.

"Iroquois" (EER uh koi) is a name given to us by others. First other Native Americans and then the French called us this. We call ourselves the *Haudenosaunee* (haw den oh SAW nee). This word means "People of the Longhouse." The Iroquois once lived in long wooden buildings called longhouses. A longhouse could be 200 feet long. As many as 20 related families lived in one house. Two families shared a sleeping area and a cooking fire. Some villages had more than 100 longhouses.

The Iroquois lands have many lakes and rivers. We used wooden canoes to travel on and fish in these lakes and rivers. When they hunted, men carried their hunting equipment in packs with wooden frames.

In this unit, you will learn more about the Iroquois and the region in which we live.

▲ The Iroquois traveled the rivers in canoes covered with tree bark. The canoes also made good shields, and they could be leaned against walls for climbing.

REVIEW Why were the forests important to the Iroquois? **Main Idea and Details**

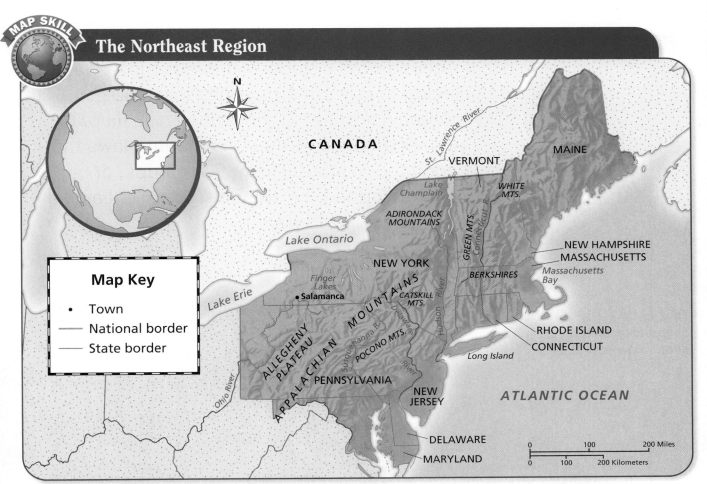

MAP SKILL

The Northeast Region

Map Key

• Town
— National border
— State border

CANADA

St. Lawrence River

MAINE

VERMONT

Lake Champlain

WHITE MTS.

ADIRONDACK MOUNTAINS

GREEN MTS.

Connecticut R.

Lake Ontario

NEW HAMPSHIRE
MASSACHUSETTS

NEW YORK

BERKSHIRES

Massachusetts Bay

Finger Lakes

• Salamanca

CATSKILL MTS.

Lake Erie

MOUNTAINS

Hudson River

Delaware R.

RHODE ISLAND
CONNECTICUT

ALLEGHENY PLATEAU

Susquehanna R.

POCONO MTS.

Long Island

APPALACHIAN

PENNSYLVANIA

NEW JERSEY

ATLANTIC OCEAN

Ohio River

DELAWARE

MARYLAND

0   100   200 Miles
0   100   200 Kilometers

▶ The Six Nations of the Iroquois lived mainly in the area that is now New York and Pennsylvania.

MAP SKILL Read a Map *What landform is most common in New York and Pennsylvania?*

History of the Iroquois

The region that is now the northeastern part of the United States was the home of several Native American groups. These groups together are called the Iroquois.

For hundreds of years, these groups fought with each other. An Iroquois legend tells how two wise leaders brought peace to the Iroquois.

Deganawida (day gahn uh WEE duh) and Hiawatha (hey e uh WAH thuh) believed the Iroquois could settle arguments without fighting. The two men went from village to village, talking to people. They explained how the lives of the people would improve if the fighting stopped. Many listened and agreed.

Around 1570, leaders of five groups—the Oneida (oh NEYE duh), Cayuga (kah YOO guh), Mohawk (MOH hawk), Onondaga (ahn un DAH guh), and Seneca—met and created laws that ended the fighting. These five groups, or nations, formed the **Iroquois League**. Later, a sixth group, the Tuscarora (tus kah ROR ah), joined the league.

▲ **Chief Joseph Brant was a respected Iroquois leader who lived during the American Revolution.**

▼ **This picture is a European artist's idea of an Iroquois meeting.**

By the late 1600s, many Europeans had settled in the region. England, France, and The Netherlands sent settlers to claim land. The settlers also wanted to trade with Native Americans for animal furs. At first, the new settlers lived peacefully with the Iroquois. Then they began taking over Iroquois land. The Iroquois resisted.

After the American Revolution, United States soldiers fought the Iroquois. The Iroquois were forced to give up much of their land. By 1800 many Iroquois had moved north to Canada.

Not all the Iroquois left the United States. Today many Iroquois live in big cities such as New York City, Buffalo, and Albany. Others live on reservations in New York State.

REVIEW Why was the Iroquois League formed? **Summarize**

Iroquois Headdresses

Men from each of the six groups in the Iroquois League wear different headdresses for important meetings. You can tell a man's group by looking at how his feathers are arranged.

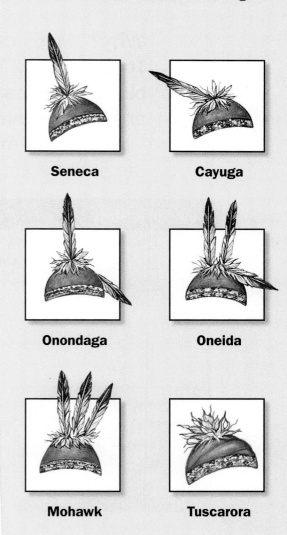

Seneca

Cayuga

Onondaga

Oneida

Mohawk

Tuscarora

Map and Globe Skills

Read Inset Maps

What? An **inset map** is a smaller map set within a larger map. Usually the inset map shows a small part of the larger map in greater detail.

Why? Maps can be used in many different ways. They can show small areas, like a street or a city block. Maps can also show large areas, like a state or an entire country.

   Look at the map of New York State. This map shows the entire state.

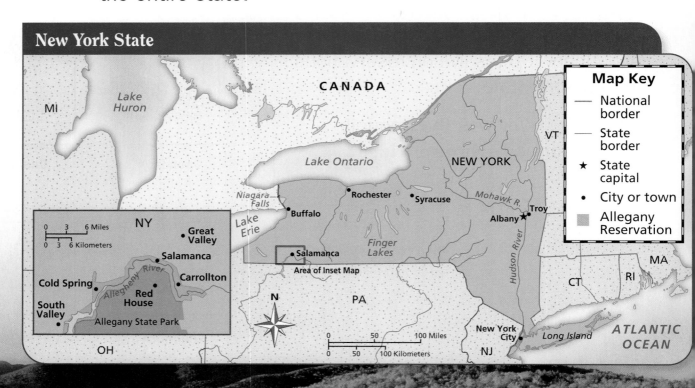

Look at the smaller map. This map shows a smaller area of western New York. It shows a much more detailed picture of the smaller area. On this map, you can see the Allegany Indian Reservation.

These two maps are useful for showing different types of information. The map of New York shows some of the state's large cities and rivers.

The inset map shows towns that are close to the reservation, such as Salamanca. It also shows the Allegheny River that runs through the reservation.

How? To find the area of the inset map, look for the rectangle on the larger map. That rectangle shows the area of the inset map in relation to the larger map. Can you see the Allegheny River on both maps?

Think and Apply

1. Which map would you use to find out about how far Cold Spring is from Salamanca? where Cold Spring is?

2. What river in New York empties into the Atlantic Ocean? Which map did you use to find this information?

3. What are the names of three other cities in New York? Which map did you use to find this information? What city shown on the map is closest to Niagara Falls?

Government of the Iroquois

Long ago, the Iroquois lived in villages made up of many longhouses. Each person in a longhouse belonged to the same clan, or group of relatives. Iroquois clans had animal names such as Turtle, Bear, Beaver, and Deer. The Iroquois did not have a written language. Elders told stories about their clan history to the younger people. An **elder** is a respected older person in a family or community. The stories told by the elders helped teach Iroquois laws and customs.

Women played a key role in Iroquois government. They made decisions about the longhouses and the use of farmland. The oldest woman in each clan was known as a clan mother. The clan mother in each clan chose the clan leader. The leaders were men. Members of each clan met in a village council. The council decided when to plant crops, build new buildings, and hold certain celebrations.

▲ These carved animals are some of the symbols of Iroquois clans.

▼ The Seneca chief known as Cornplanter led the Iroquois League at the time of the American Revolution.

▼ Cyrus Schindler was president of the Seneca people at the beginning of the 21st century.

All Iroquois villages were part of the Iroquois League. The members of the league chose 50 leaders to represent them in the Grand Council. They called these leaders **sachems** (SAY chems). The Iroquois also had a constitution, which served as a basis for parts of the Constitution of the United States.

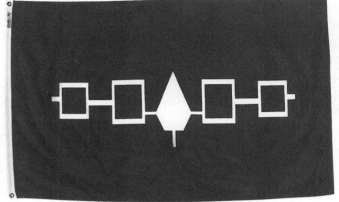

▲ The flag of the Iroquois Grand Council

The Grand Council met in the land of the Onondaga. This was near the center of the Iroquois lands. They planned festivals, settled arguments, and decided when war was necessary or peace was possible. During these meetings, each person had a chance to speak. Sometimes sachems talked for days until they made up their minds. No decision was final until all 50 leaders agreed.

Today the Iroquois have two grand councils. One council meets in Canada. The other council meets on the Onondaga reservation near Syracuse, New York. Sometimes both grand councils meet together to discuss common problems.

REVIEW What kinds of decisions did the Grand Council make? **Summarize**

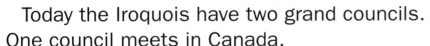

▶ This is how the Iroquois Constitution begins.

The Constitution of the Iroquois Nations

The Great Binding Law, Gayanashagowa

1. I am Dekanawidah and with the Five Nations' Confederate Lords I plant the Tree of Great Peace. I plant it in your territory, Adodarhoh, and the Onondaga Nation, in the territory of you who are Firekeepers. I name the tree the Tree of the Great Long Leaves. Under the shade of this Tree of the Great Peace we spread the soft white feathery down of the globe thistle as seats for you, Adodarhoh, and your cousin Lords. We place you upon those seats, spread soft with the feathery down of the globe thistle, there beneath the shade of the spreading branches of the Tree of Peace. There shall you sit and watch the Council Fire of the Confederacy of the Five Nations, and all the affairs of the Five Nations shall be transacted at this place before you, Adodarhoh, and your cousin Lords, by the Confederate Lords of the Five Nations.

▲ The Iroquois always planted corn, beans, and squash together.

Economy of the Iroquois

Each member of an Iroquois household had an important job to do. Men hunted, fished, and cleared the forests. Young boys learned from their fathers. Women planted and harvested the crops. Young girls helped their mothers in the fields and cared for younger children. They also helped with cooking and cleaning.

The Iroquois depended on farming for most of their food. They planted corn, beans, and squash. They called these crops the Three Sisters. As the squash and bean plants grew, they wrapped around the cornstalks. This made it easier to dig out weeds and harvest the crops.

The Iroquois traded with the Huron and other Native American groups. The Iroquois gave the Huron such goods as dried fish and pipes carved from stone. In return the Huron gave them shells and copper.

▼ Europeans traded with the Iroquois for beaver and other animal skins. They sent them back to Europe, where beaver hats were very popular.

Trade with Europeans changed the Iroquois way of life. Traders brought guns, pots, tools, jewelry, glass beads, and clothing. They traded these goods with the Iroquois in exchange for furs. In time, the Iroquois stopped making their own weapons and tools. They began to use European goods.

Today the Iroquois work in many different jobs. Some work as teachers, doctors, and carpenters. Others make and sell traditional Iroquois crafts, such as baskets and pottery. On the Allegany Reservation, many people work for the government of the Seneca Nation or in businesses owned by the Seneca.

▼ The Iroquois still make and use pottery.

REVIEW What caused the economy of the Iroquois to change? **Cause and Effect**

◀ Onondaga artist Oren Lyons completes a painting of the Tree of Peace.

Culture of the Iroquois

▲ This is Iroquois cornbread. The Iroquois made many dishes from corn. They boiled it, roasted it on the cob, and baked it. Sometimes they sweetened corn flour with sap from maple trees.

Many Iroquois festivals celebrated the importance of farming. Corn-planting and corn-gathering festivals were held at different times of the year. There were also strawberry and maple sugar festivals. The Iroquois still gather for some of these celebrations today.

Each winter the Iroquois hold a Midwinter Festival to celebrate the New Year. During the Midwinter Festival long ago, families cleaned out their longhouses. They put out old cooking fires. At the end of the festival, they lit new fires. The festival celebrates a new beginning.

FACT FILE

Iroquois Festivals

The Iroquois have many festivals or ceremonies throughout the year. What holidays do Americans have today to celebrate harvests or the beginning of a new year?

Festival	Month	Occasion
Midwinter Festival	January	Celebrates the New Year
All Night Dance	March	Honors the dead
Sun Dance	May	Gives thanks to the sun for helping plants grow
Green Bean Dance	July	Gives thanks for beans, one of the Three Sisters
Harvest Dance	October	Celebrates the end of the harvest

Members of the Six Nations meet every year for the Iroquois Festival. This festival has been held for more than 20 years near the Iroquois Indian Museum in Howes Cave, New York. At this and other festivals, people share arts and crafts, eat traditional foods, and listen to storytellers. Children have fun making corn-husk dolls. These festivals are one way that the Iroquois share their culture today.

The Seneca-Iroquois Nation Museum is in Salamanca, New York. Visitors can watch Seneca artists make cow-horn rattles or moccasins like their ancestors did long ago.

▲ Cornhusk dolls

REVIEW Describe two important Iroquois traditions. **Summarize**

▲ Iroquois child's mocassins

▼ The Iroquois built longhouse roofs with holes so smoke from fires could escape.

DIAGRAM SKILL *How did the Iroquois reach the storage in the longhouse?*

Clothes made of animal skins

Animal-skin curtain for privacy

Smoke Hole

Storage

Beds

Bark Walls

Frame

Ladder

Fire

Entrance

27

Review

1. What is the climate like in the Northeast?

2. How did belonging to the Iroquois League change the way the member nations lived?

3. What did the Iroquois trade with other Native American groups?

4. What part did women play in the government of the Iroquois?

5. Describe how leaders in the Grand Council made decisions in their meetings. When was a decision final?

6. What type of jobs did Iroquois boys and girls have?

7. **Use an Inset Map** Look at the map on page 20. What three cities or towns can you find in the Allegany Indian Reservation?

Link to ∞ Writing

Write an Article: Suppose you are a newspaper reporter writing about the Iroquois today. Write a one-paragraph article describing how the Iroquois celebrate their culture today.

Test Talk

Strategy 3
Choose the Right Answer

Directions: Sometimes a question asks you to choose the best answer. Follow these steps.

- Read the question.
- Read each answer choice.
- Cross out answer choices that you know are wrong.
- Mark your answer choice.
- Check your answer. Compare your answer to the text.

Try It Cross out answer choices that you know are wrong. Mark your answer choice. Then check your answer.

1. Who chose Iroquois clan leaders?
   - **A.** Sachems
   - **B.** Women
   - **C.** Children
   - **D.** Grand Council

2. What crops were most important to the Iroquois?
   - **A.** Corn, rice, and melons
   - **B.** Beans, wheat, and squash
   - **C.** Corn, beans, and squash
   - **D.** Apples, beans, and rice

These projects will help you learn about other Native American groups.

Native American Sports

Make a booklet. Throughout North America, Native American groups had many kinds of games of skill. These games included spear throwing, racing, juggling, and ball games. One of the most popular games throughout the Eastern Woodlands was lacrosse. It is still played today. Find out how lacrosse or another Native American game was played long ago. Make a booklet, explaining how and why the game was played. Include pictures. Share your booklet with the class.

Living on the Coast

Make a diorama. In the Northeast, many Native American groups lived along the Atlantic Ocean. These groups fished for some of their food. They also gathered shellfish. Learn more about one of these groups and create a diorama showing how this group lived. Be sure to include some of the spears, nets, and traps they used to catch fish.

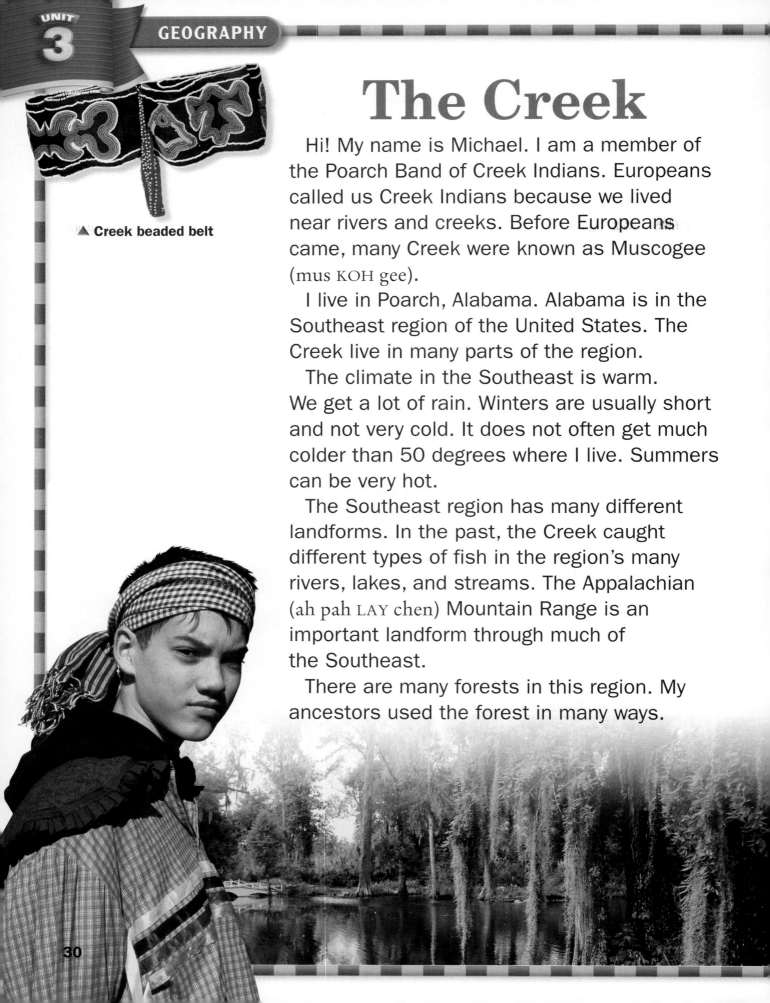

▲ Creek beaded belt

The Creek

Hi! My name is Michael. I am a member of the Poarch Band of Creek Indians. Europeans called us Creek Indians because we lived near rivers and creeks. Before Europeans came, many Creek were known as Muscogee (mus KOH gee).

I live in Poarch, Alabama. Alabama is in the Southeast region of the United States. The Creek live in many parts of the region.

The climate in the Southeast is warm. We get a lot of rain. Winters are usually short and not very cold. It does not often get much colder than 50 degrees where I live. Summers can be very hot.

The Southeast region has many different landforms. In the past, the Creek caught different types of fish in the region's many rivers, lakes, and streams. The Appalachian (ah pah LAY chen) Mountain Range is an important landform through much of the Southeast.

There are many forests in this region. My ancestors used the forest in many ways.

Men used wood and bark from the trees to build the roofs of their houses. Women gathered wild berries and nuts that grew in the forest.

Many animals live in the Southeast. In some places you will see bears, beavers, raccoons, deer, rabbits, and squirrels. Long ago, the Creek hunted many of these animals for food and fur.

Read on to learn more about the Creek people and the Southeast region.

REVIEW Describe the climate of the Southeast. **Summarize**

▲ **This picture of a Creek house was drawn in 1757.**

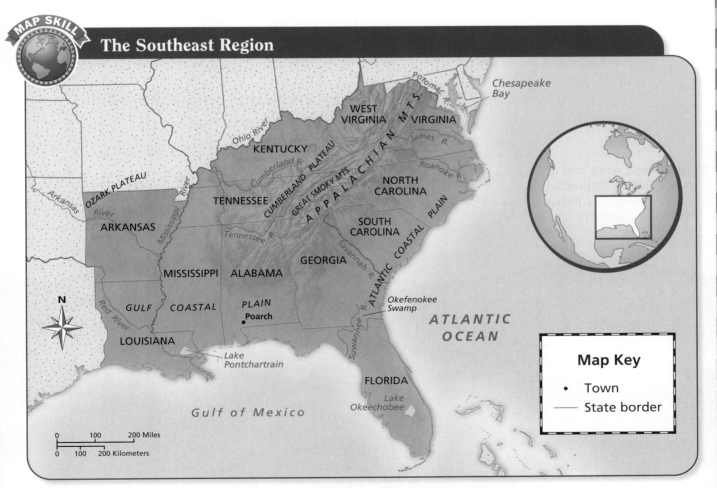

MAP SKILL

The Southeast Region

Map Key
- • Town
- — State border

▶ In the 1500s, most Creek Indians lived in what is now Georgia and Alabama.

MAP SKILL Location *What other state is Poarch, Alabama, closest to?*

History of the Creek

The Creek have lived for a very long time in the area that is now Alabama and Georgia. Do you remember reading about the Mississippian people in Unit 1? The Mississippian people were the ancestors of the Creek Indians. Some Creek Indians lived in or near Moundville. Early Creek artifacts are similar to Mississippian artifacts. Early Creek people worked with seashells and copper and made beads and pottery.

In 1540 the first European to make contact with the Creek was a Spanish explorer. His name was **Hernando de Soto** (her NAN doh de SOH toh). During the next 200 years, settlers from England, France, and Spain came to the Southeast. These settlers were looking for good farmland.

At first, these new settlers and the Native Americans agreed to share the land. Later, the settlers decided they wanted the land for themselves. Many Native American groups in

▲ The Creek made this necklace of carved seashells.

▼ The Creek were one of many Native American groups forced to move to Indian Territory.

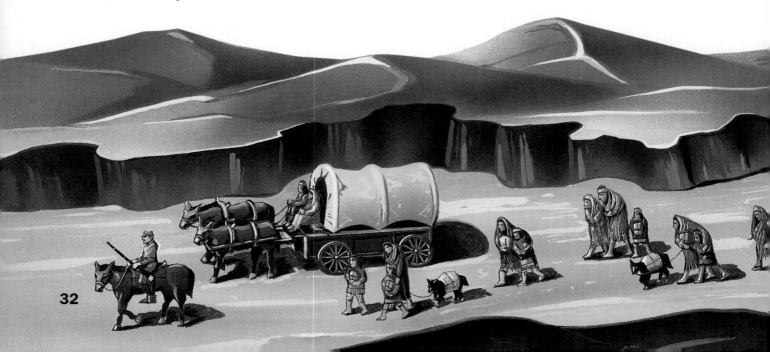

32

the region, including the Creek, worked together to resist the settlers and the changes they brought.

The U.S. government decided to move the Creek and other Native Americans from the land. The Native Americans did not want to move. In 1838 United States soldiers began to force the Creek and other groups to move west to a place called Indian Territory. Many people died on the long, difficult journey. This journey became known as the Trail of Tears.

Indian Territory became the state of Oklahoma. Many Creek still live in Oklahoma today. However, not all the Creek moved to Indian Territory. Some, like the Poarch Band of Creek Indians, stayed behind.

▲ **Creek pottery jar**

REVIEW Describe the events leading to the Trail of Tears. **Summarize**

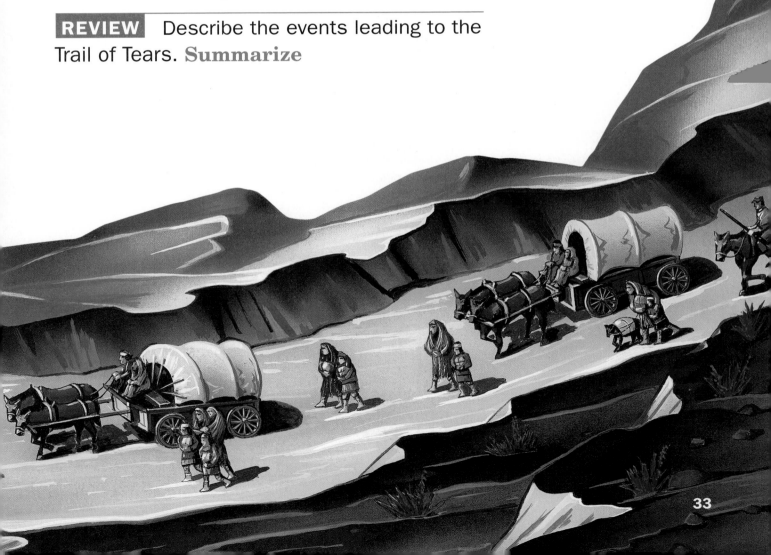

Map and Globe Skills

Read a History Map

What? A **history map** can show different things about the past. It may show how countries or continents were divided. It may show where places were located long ago.

Why? History maps help us understand more about the past. This history map shows the United States around the time Native Americans in the Southeast were moved to the Southwest. They were moved into the part of the Unorganized Territory that is now Oklahoma. On this map, you can see which

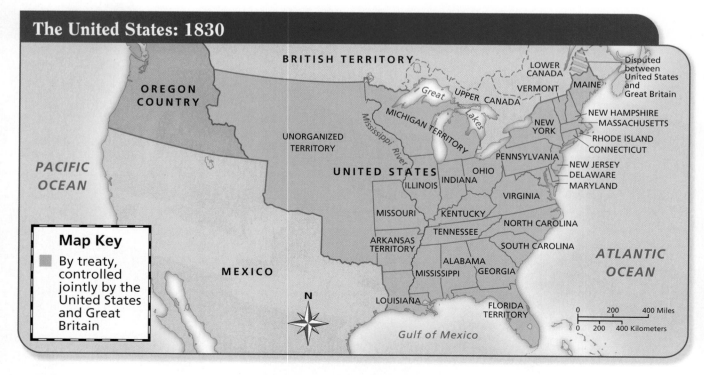

The United States: 1830

BRITISH TERRITORY

OREGON COUNTRY

UNORGANIZED TERRITORY

PACIFIC OCEAN

MEXICO

N

LOWER CANADA

VERMONT

Great Lakes

UPPER CANADA

MICHIGAN TERRITORY

Mississippi River

UNITED STATES

ILLINOIS

INDIANA

OHIO

MISSOURI

KENTUCKY

ARKANSAS TERRITORY

TENNESSEE

MISSISSIPPI

ALABAMA

LOUISIANA

GEORGIA

SOUTH CAROLINA

NORTH CAROLINA

VIRGINIA

PENNSYLVANIA

NEW YORK

MAINE

Disputed between United States and Great Britain

NEW HAMPSHIRE

MASSACHUSETTS

RHODE ISLAND

CONNECTICUT

NEW JERSEY

DELAWARE

MARYLAND

ATLANTIC OCEAN

FLORIDA TERRITORY

Gulf of Mexico

Map Key

By treaty, controlled jointly by the United States and Great Britain

0   200   400 Miles
0   200   400 Kilometers

states were part of the United States in 1830. Some of the states did not have the same borders that they have today. Much of the land west of the Mississippi River was not organized into the states that we know today. Some parts of the country were called territories. A **territory** is land that belongs to the government. Mexico claimed a large part of what is now the United States. Much of the country was still being explored and settled.

How? Each color helps you understand the map. The color green shows the states and territories that were part of the United States. Other colors show other parts of North America. Mexico is gold on the map. What does the color orange show?

Think and Apply

1 What can a **history map** show?

2 Besides the unorganized **territory**, name three other territories shown on this map.

3 What states bordered the Arkansas Territory?

Government of the Creek

In the past, the Creek lived in villages. Every person in a Creek village belonged to a clan. As you read in Unit 2, a clan is a group of people who are all related. The members of each clan share an ancestor. Creek children belonged to the same clan as their mother. The children learned from the adults in the clan. Like the Iroquois, each clan was named after an animal. Some of the clans were named the Alligator Clan, the Bird Clan, and the Deer Clan.

Creek villages were organized into red towns and white towns. People who lived in red towns were ready to fight to protect their village. People who lived in white towns were peacekeepers. They worked to help others.

Each town chose leaders to be part of a council. Each Creek council chose a chief to be their leader.

▶ **Many Creek are also known as Muscogee. This is their official seal. The seal shows pictures of wheat and a plow.**

▼ **Many Creek villages were built beside rivers.**

36

Creek Confederacy

Executive Branch
- Principal Chief
- Second Chief
- Executive Director

Legislative Branch
- Council of Representatives

Judicial Branch
- Supreme Court
- Chief Justice
- District Court Judges

◀ Like the United States, the Creek Confederacy has three branches of government.

All of the Creek towns were part of the Creek Confederacy (con FEHD er ah see). A **confederacy** is made up of groups that join together for support or for a special purpose. Each town chief represented his town at meetings of the Creek Confederacy. The chiefs of the confederacy met once a year to solve problems, plan festivals, and decide when to go to war or make peace.

Many Creek live in the United States today. Councils still meet to discuss problems and make decisions. The councils are still part of the Creek Confederacy. Today they meet in Okmulgee (oak MUHL gee), a town in eastern Oklahoma.

The Poarch Band of Creek Indians has their own government. It is a separate government from the Creek Nation. Their government is in Alabama.

REVIEW What happened at the yearly meeting of the Creek Confederacy?
Main Idea and Details

▼ Marian McCormick is the principle chief of the Lower Muscogee Creek.

37

Economy of the Creek

The early Creek depended on farming, hunting, and fishing in order to live. There were important jobs to do all year long.

In the spring the men cleared the fields and the women planted seeds. Girls learned how to plant when they were very young. They helped their mothers. Together they planted corn, beans, squash, pumpkins, and melons.

While Creek women were planting, the men were hunting or fishing. Boys learned how to hunt from their fathers. It was easy to find fish and shellfish in the rivers and streams that were near most villages. During the spring, the Creek hunted small animals in nearby forests. These animals included raccoons, opossums, and turkeys. In the fall and winter, the men would travel far from their villages to look for larger animals. Most of their meat came from deer. They also hunted bears and bison, or buffalo. The Creek who lived in what is now Florida also hunted alligators.

▲ Wood and a seashell are tied together to make an adze, a tool used to shape large pieces of wood.

◄ This Creek hunter carries his traditional bow and arrows and spear. He also carries a gun, which he would have gotten from a European trader.

The Creek made many of the things they used every day. Pots were made from clay. Weapons were made from wood or stone. The Creek also wove baskets. When Europeans began to arrive, they brought metal pots and tools. They also brought fishhooks and guns. The Europeans traded these things with the Creek for animal furs.

Today many Creek earn their livings the same way others in this country do. Some members of the Poarch Band of Creek Indians are farmers. Some are doctors or teachers. Others work in factories, in hotels, and at many other jobs.

REVIEW What did Creek women and girls do to get the food they needed? What did Creek men and boys do?
Main Idea and Details

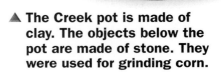

▲ The Creek pot is made of clay. The objects below the pot are made of stone. They were used for grinding corn.

▼ Today the Creek work at many different jobs, such as being police officers.

Culture of the Creek

Every Creek town was built around a plaza (PLAH zah). A **plaza** is a public square in a city or town. The leaders held meetings in the plaza around a special fire. The fire burned all year long. The Creek also met in the plaza to play games. Ceremonies and festivals were also held there.

The most important festival of the year was the Green Corn Festival. This festival was held in summer, when the corn first ripens. The Creek cleaned their houses to get ready for the festival. They also threw away old clothes and any cracked or broken dishes. It was a time for everything to begin again.

The Creek gathered to feast on corn and other types of food. There were games and contests. Special dances were performed. The fire in the plaza was put out at the beginning of the Green Corn Festival and lit again before the big feast.

▼ Part of the Creek Green Corn Festival took place in the town plaza.

40

Festivals and celebrations are an important part of Creek life today. Many Creek still celebrate the Green Corn Festival. So do other groups in the Southeast. These groups include the Cherokee (chair OH kee) and the Seminole (SEH min ohl). At the Green Corn Festival, people enjoy a big feast. The feast includes roasted corn, corn soup, cornbread, and other foods made from corn.

The Muscogee Creek in Oklahoma hold the Creek Nation Festival every year in June. The festival includes a rodeo. The Poarch Band of Creek Indians has a big festival every year on Thanksgiving Day. Traditional dances are performed at this festival. People wear traditional clothing too. It is a time to remember their history and to keep their culture alive.

REVIEW How do the Creek celebrate the Green Corn Festival?

Main Idea and Details

▲ Traditional festivals help keep Creek culture alive and pass it down from parents to children and grandchildren.

FACT FILE

Creek Language Today

The Creek language is still spoken by many Creek people. Think about some things people say every day. You can say them in Creek!

Heres ce (HINS chay)	Hello
Mvdo (MUH do)	Thank you
Inka (IN gah)	Okay!; All right!
Monks (MONKS)	No
Hvtec ce (hah dich KAY)	Wait!

1. How did the Creek get their name?

2. Who was the first European to make contact with the Creek?

3. What was the Trail of Tears?

4. What is a confederacy? Who are members of the Creek Confederacy?

5. Name three ways the Creek used the town plaza.

6. What was the most important festival of the year for the Creek?

7. **Use a History Map** Look at the map on page 35. Look at a map of the United States today. Describe two ways that the maps are different.

Link to — Writing

Write a Journal Entry: Suppose you were growing up in a Creek village long ago. Write a journal entry describing your day. Include things you have seen, work you have done, and things you have learned to do.

Test Talk

**Strategy 2
Locate Key Words in the Text.**

Directions: Think about where you need to look for an answer. Follow these steps.

- Read the question.
- Look for and circle key words in the question.
- Look for and circle key words in the text that match key words in the question.
- Decide where to look for the answer.
    To find the answer, you may have to **look in one place in the text.**
    To find the answer, you may have to **look in several places in the text.**
    To find the answer, you may have to **combine what you know with what the author tells you.**

Try It Copy the question below on a separate sheet of paper. Circle the key words in the question.

What types of animals live in the Southeast?

Copy the sentence below on the same sheet of paper. Fill in the blanks.

I found the answer on page ___, paragraph ___, sentence ___.

Projects

These projects will help you learn about other Native American groups.

Native American Legends

Learn about a legend. Many Native Americans have legends that tell stories about past people or events. Legends are one way that people pass on values, ideas, beliefs, and traditions. Form a group. Research a Native American legend. Assign parts to act out or read aloud the legend to your class.

Map It!

Draw a map. Research the geography of the Southeast region of the United States. Draw a map that shows the landforms and the bodies of water in the region. Include a map key.

The Lakota

Hello, my name is Andrew. I am a member of the Oglala (o GLA la) Indian Nation. I live with my family on the Pine Ridge Reservation in South Dakota.

The Oglala are one of many groups that belong to the Lakota branch of the Sioux (SOO) Nation. All the Lakota speak the same language. In our language the word *Lakota* means "friend."

The Lakota lands are in the western part of the Midwest region of the United States. The Midwest is mostly flat, but the Lakota lands are different. Part of our lands are in an area called the Black Hills. Another part of our lands are in an area called the Badlands. These areas are not flat.

The Black Hills are beautiful mountains. They are covered with forests of pine trees. From a distance, the forests look black. That is why my ancestors called them the Black Hills.

The Badlands are beautiful. They are called the Badlands because they are hard to travel across. The climate is very dry. There are few plants. But the rocks are colorful and have been carved into wonderful shapes.

▲ Only warriors who were great in battle wore headdresses, which are also known as warbonnets. The war chiefs had the longest warbonnets.

The shapes were made over thousands of years by erosion. **Erosion** is when wind and rain wear away the rock a little at a time.

Today the Oglala help preserve Badlands National Park. Park visitors see buffalo, elk, antelope, and other animals. These animals have lived in the Midwest region for thousands of years.

Read on to learn more about the Lakota people and the Midwest region.

▲ **The Badlands have been shaped by erosion.**

REVIEW What two areas of the Midwest region make up Lakota lands?

Main Idea and Details

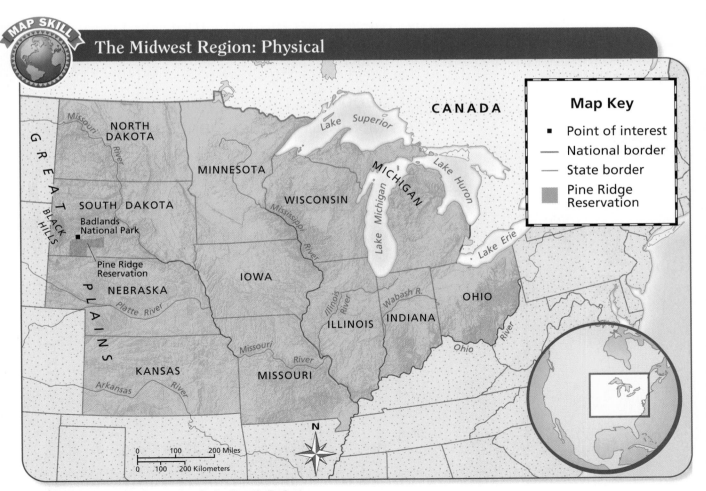

The Midwest Region: Physical

Map Key

- ▪ Point of interest
- — National border
- — State border
- ▪ Pine Ridge Reservation

CANADA

NORTH DAKOTA

MINNESOTA

SOUTH DAKOTA
Badlands National Park
Pine Ridge Reservation

NEBRASKA

IOWA

WISCONSIN

MICHIGAN

Lake Superior

Lake Huron

Lake Michigan

Lake Erie

OHIO

INDIANA

ILLINOIS

KANSAS

MISSOURI

GREAT PLAINS

BLACK HILLS

Missouri River

Mississippi River

Platte River

Illinois River

Wabash R.

Ohio River

Missouri River

Arkansas River

0   100   200 Miles
0   100   200 Kilometers

N

▲ **Pine Ridge Reservation is in South Dakota.**

MAP SKILL Understand Borders: *What state borders on the southern part of the Pine Ridge Reservation?*

45

History of the Lakota

For generations the Lakota people moved from place to place. They moved because they were following herds of buffalo. The buffalo were very important to the Lakota. You will read why on pages 50–51.

The Lakota wanted to remember their history. Every winter they painted pictures of the year's most important events on a buffalo skin. They called these painted skins the winter count.

The Lakota came to the Black Hills in the 1600s. They saw it was a good place to live. The Black Hills had plenty of water to drink. The land was beautiful. There were buffalo nearby. The Lakota also felt that the Great Spirit of their religion lived in the Black Hills. They decided to settle in the Black Hills.

When Europeans began to arrive, many changes occurred. Some changes helped

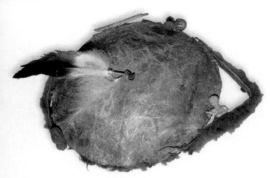

▲ This shield is made of buffalo hide.

▼ Pictures on this winter count of houses and people in non-native clothes show that Europeans had arrived by the time this was painted.

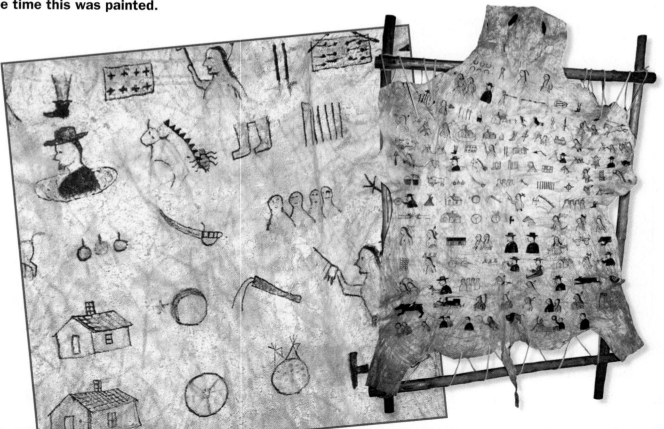

46

the Lakota. The introduction of the horse made travel easier. The Lakota also traded with Europeans. But Europeans killed many buffalo. This hurt the Lakota.

In the 1800s the United States government forced the Lakota to give up much of their land. The United States Army made the Lakota move onto reservations. Today most Lakota live on reservations in North Dakota, South Dakota, and Nebraska. The largest Lakota Reservation is the Pine Ridge Reservation in South Dakota.

Museums such as the Red Cloud Heritage Center and the Crazy Horse Memorial help celebrate Lakota history. Visitors can view traditional Lakota clothing and artifacts, as well as many paintings, photographs, and sculptures of people and events.

▲ This photograph of the Pine Ridge Reservation was taken in 1891.

▼ The Crazy Horse Memorial is being built in honor of one of the Lakota's most famous leaders, Tasunke Witko, or Crazy Horse. He was a great warrior and worked to preserve the Lakota way of life.

REVIEW   Why did the Lakota decide to settle in the Black Hills?
Cause and Effect

47

Government of the Lakota

Long ago, Lakota families traveled together in bands. A **band** is a group of families that live together. Everyone in the band helped to maintain law and order. Lakota children were taught at a very early age how to behave. They were expected to help the band and keep the laws even when they were young.

▲ The Lakota traditionally set up their tepees in a circle. Everyone in camp had work to do.

Each band chose a respected man to be its chief. The chief led council meetings. The council was made up of elders, warriors, and other respected members of the band. The council worked with the chief to make decisions, such as when and where to move. If everyone disagreed with a chief, a new chief could be selected. If one person or one family disagreed, they could leave and join another band.

Within every band, some people belonged to societies, or groups that met to work on specific needs in the band. Men and women belonged to separate societies. Some societies helped sick people. Other societies created dances for ceremonies. Many young men joined a warrior society when they were 16 years old. These young men helped defend the Lakota from enemies. Men who were brave and skilled in battle gained status within the band.

Today each Lakota reservation has its own separate government. The people on the Pine Ridge Reservation have a tribal council for their government. There are 18 members of the tribal council. Members of the council are elected every four years. Council members work together to make important decisions, such as where to build schools and roads.

The Pine Ridge Reservation is divided into eight districts. These are represented by the eight tepees on the Oglala flag.

▲ This is the flag of the Oglala of the Pine Ridge Reservation.

REVIEW What was the purpose of Lakota societies? **Main Idea and Details**

▼ Bravery is still valued among the Lakota. Lakota veterans from the United States armed forces have places of honor at gatherings.

Economy of the Lakota

▲ The Lakota made items such as this bag both for personal use and for trade. The bag is made of buffalo skin decorated with colored porcupine quills.

For generations the economy of the Lakota was based on buffalo hunting. The buffalo provided almost everything the people needed. Buffalo meat provided food. Buffalo skins provided clothing and shelter. The Lakota tied dried buffalo skins around wooden poles to make homes called tepees. Tepees were easy to move.

The buffalo provided other useful things as well. Besides clothes and tepees, buffalo skin was used to make pouches, rope, and shields. Buffalo hides, or skin with the hair still on it, made warm robes and blankets. Buffalo horns were carved into cups and spoons. Tools were made from the bones.

Buffalo herds wandered the Great Plains and searched for grass to eat. The Lakota traveled constantly to hunt them. The Lakota followed the buffalo on foot, bringing all they needed with them. Each family piled their belongings onto a wooden sled called a travois (tra VOY). A dog pulled each travois. This made traveling easier.

FACT FILE

Lakota Horses

Spanish explorers brought horses to North America in the 1500s. Plains Indians such as the Lakota learned how to tame and ride horses from other groups of Native Americans. Because they had never seen horses before, the Lakota had no word for *horse*. They called horses "sacred dogs" because they were even more important and useful than the dogs they had.

◀ A dog was used to pull the travois before horses were known to the Lakota.

In the 1700s horses became very important to the Lakota. Horses had been brought to North America by Europeans. The Lakota got their horses by trading with other Native American groups. Horses made hunting buffalo much easier. The Lakota could then travel farther and faster. A horse could also pull a larger travois.

After the Lakota settled in the Black Hills, they became great traders. They traded their buffalo products with other Native American groups for corn and other crops. They also traded with European settlers. In return they received metal tools, guns, and other trade goods.

Today the Lakota people work at many different jobs. Most are farmers or ranchers. Some are teachers or lawyers; some are artists or construction workers. Many travel from the Pine Ridge Reservation to Rapid City, South Dakota, to work.

▼ A Sioux business man draws diagrams during a business meeting.

REVIEW How was the buffalo important to the Lakota economy?

Main Idea and Details

Culture of the Lakota

The Lakota have always celebrated their rich culture through art, special ceremonies, and music. These celebrations continue today.

For many generations, the Lakota made paints from plants and animal oils. They used buffalo-horn paintbrushes to decorate their tepees with pictures and designs. Sometimes these paintings told a story about the owner of the tepee. As you saw on page 50, the Lakota also used colored porcupine quills to create pictures. They were famous for this beautiful "quillwork."

Art is still important to the Lakota. Every year the Red Cloud Heritage Center holds an art show. It is one of the largest Native American art shows in the country.

▲ Like other Sioux, the Lakota lived in tepees. In fact, *tepee* is a Sioux word.

▶ This painting on buffalo skin shows a Sun Dance ceremony. It was painted in the 1800s.

The Lakota also have special ceremonies. One of the most important Lakota ceremonies is the Sun Dance. The Sun Dance celebrates the Sioux way of life. The dance can last from four to eight days. Long ago, members of Plains Indian groups met once a year for the Sun Dance. These gatherings helped keep peace among them. Today the Oglala at Pine Ridge and other groups continue to celebrate the Sun Dance.

Many Lakota children learn about their culture at home and at school. Some children might choose to learn dancing or painting. Others might learn to play the drum and sing traditional songs. Not only does this help children appreciate their culture, it makes it possible for them to share it with others.

▲ A Lakota drum

REVIEW Why are art and music important in Lakota culture? **Draw Conclusions**

▼ Singers play the drum while performing traditional songs.

53

Skill Lesson: Read a Time Line

What? A **time line** shows when different events happened. It puts events in order from earliest to latest. A time line clearly labels an event and the date when it took place.

Why? Time lines help us organize events in a way that is easy to understand. Time lines show the order in which events happened. They are tools that make learning about the past easier.

How? Look at the time line on the next page. It shows events that have taken place during the creation of the Crazy Horse Memorial in South Dakota. Crazy Horse was a great Lakota chief. The memorial honors his memory.

Notice that the time line is broken into **decades**, or periods of ten years. The earliest events appear on the left side of the time line. The most recent, or latest, events appear on the right. By looking at the number of decades, we learn that the time period covered is about 60 years. Specific dates on the time line show important events. For example, the information at 1946 on the time line shows that this was the year that a spot was chosen for the memorial. The next date on the time line is 1949, which is three years later. What happened then?

Creating the Crazy Horse Memorial

1939
Lakota chiefs ask artist Korczak Ziolkowski to carve a sculpture of Crazy Horse.

1951
Korczak paints an outline of Crazy Horse on mountain.

1976
More than five million tons of rock have been removed from the mountain.

1998
The face of Crazy Horse is finished.

930 — 1940 — 1950 — 1960 — 1970 — 1980 — 1990 — 2000

1946
Korczak and Lakota leaders choose Thunderhead Mountain for the memorial.

1949
Korczak starts dynamiting the mountain to begin the carving.

1982
Korczak dies. His family carries on his work.

2000
Work continues on the monument.

Think and Apply

1. What is the purpose of a time line?

2. When did Lakota chiefs ask Korczak to build the monument?

3. Did Korczak die before or after the face of Crazy Horse was finished?

4. How much time passed between the first event on the time line and the beginning of the carving of the monument?

1. In what area of the country do many Lakota still live today?

2. Why did the early Lakota travel from place to place?

3. Compare and contrast the traditional Lakota council with the Lakota council today.

4. What role did trade play in the Lakota economy?

5. Why is the Sun Dance important in Lakota culture?

6. **Use a Time Line** Make a list of five important things that have happened in your life, such as your birthday and when you started going to school. Make a time line to show these events.

Link to ⊸∞ Writing

Write a Letter: Think about how the Lakota used the buffalo in their everyday lives. Write a letter to a friend explaining the many useful things buffalo provided for the Lakota.

Test Talk

Strategy 4: Use Information from the Text

Directions: You can use details from the text to answer questions. Follow these steps.

- Read the question.
- Look for and circle key words in the question.
- Find details in the text that answer the question. Make notes about the details.
- Reread the question and your notes. Cross out notes that do not match the question. Add details, if needed.

Try It Use information from the text to answer the question. Write your answer on a separate sheet of paper.

1. Why were buffalo important to the Lakota?

These projects will help you learn about other Native American groups.

Art in the Great Plains

Make a deck of animal cards. The Native Americans of the Midwest depended on many animals. For example, they hunted buffalo and deer. What other animals were important to them? Form a group to find out. Then write the name of each animal on a note card. Draw a picture of the animal. Write down two facts about the animal on the back of the card.

Shelter

Make a model. Long ago the Lakota and other Plains Indian groups lived in tepees because they were easy to move. Make a model of a tepee. Find pictures of tepees in this book, in other books, or on the Internet to get ideas of how to decorate your model. Share your model with the class. Explain to the class how you decorated your tepee and what symbols you used.

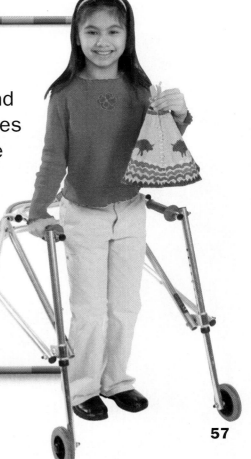

The Navajo

Hello, my name is Jill. I am a member of the Navajo (NAH vah hoh) Nation. I live with my family in Window Rock, Arizona. Window Rock is on the Navajo Reservation. The Navajo Reservation covers parts of Arizona, New Mexico, and Utah.

The Navajo Reservation is near a part of the United States called the Four Corners. This is where the borders of four states meet. The four states are Utah, Colorado, New Mexico, and Arizona. The Navajo, including my relatives, have lived in this area for hundreds of years.

My state of Arizona is in the Southwest region. I like the Southwest very much because it has many different landforms. You can visit mountains and canyons. **Canyons** are deep valleys with high, steep sides. Most of the region is dry and hot in the summer. It seldom rains. Many parts of the Southwest have mild winters. The Navajo Reservation is in an area called the Colorado Plateau. A **plateau** is a high, flat area. The winters there are cold and snowy.

Like the Iroquois, many of my Navajo ancestors were farmers. They planted crops in low-lying land such as valleys and canyons.

▲ The town of Window Rock is named for this unusual rock formation.

These low areas held water from the rain. Canyon walls provided protection from the wind.

My ancestors did not live in a house that looks like the one I live in. They lived in dwellings called hogans. Hogans are one-room houses with as many as eight sides. Some hogans have thick walls. These walls help to keep the inside of the hogan warm. Some Navajo still live in hogans today.

The Navajo call themselves Diné (dee NAY), which means "The People." As you read more, you will see how the Diné live and work.

▲ A Navajo hogan

REVIEW Describe the land of the Navajo Reservation. **Main Idea and Details**

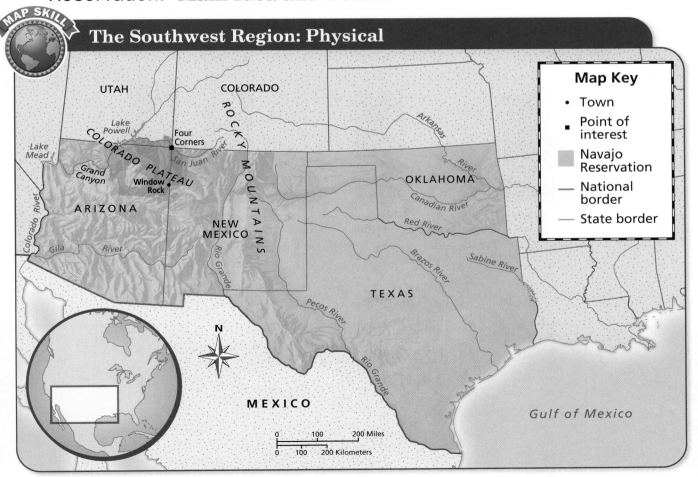

The Southwest Region: Physical

Map Key
- Town
- ▪ Point of interest
- ▨ Navajo Reservation
- — National border
- — State border

UTAH · COLORADO · Lake Powell · Four Corners · ROCKY MOUNTAINS · Arkansas River · Lake Mead · COLORADO PLATEAU · San Juan River · OKLAHOMA · Grand Canyon · Window Rock · Canadian River · Colorado River · ARIZONA · NEW MEXICO · Red River · Gila River · Rio Grande · Brazos River · Sabine River · TEXAS · Pecos River · Rio Grande · N · MEXICO · Gulf of Mexico

0   100   200 Miles
0   100   200 Kilometers

▲ Most of the Navajo Reservation is in Arizona.

MAP SKILL Use a Compass Rose *Which state in this region is farthest west? farthest south?*

59

Bar Graphs

What? A **bar graph** uses bars to show information. It shows facts in a clear, simple picture. This graph shows the average amount of rainfall in six cities in one year.

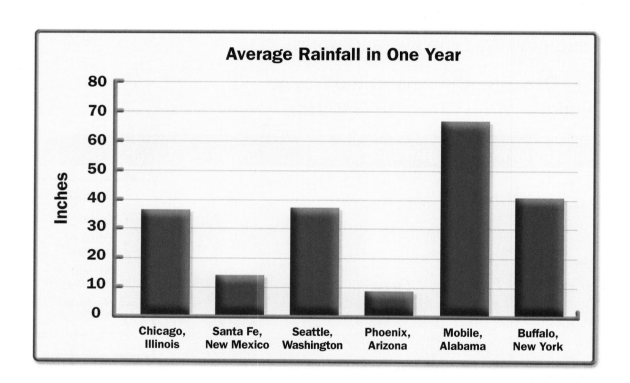

Average Rainfall in One Year

(Inches, from 0 to 80)

Chicago, Illinois	
Santa Fe, New Mexico	
Seattle, Washington	
Phoenix, Arizona	
Mobile, Alabama	
Buffalo, New York	

Why? Bar graphs help you find information quickly and easily. They also help you compare information.

For example, different regions of the United States have different kinds of climates. The amount of rain that falls is an important part of an area's climate. In some places a lot of rain falls each year. In other places it is very dry. If you want to compare the rainfall in different places, you might use a bar graph.

How? First, read the title of the graph and the labels on the graph. This information tells you what the graph is showing. Then look at the bar graph. The numbers along the side tell you the number of inches of rainfall. The names at the bottom tell you where the rain was measured. Follow the bar for the city of Santa Fe to where it stops. Now look across at the inches column to learn the average number of inches of rainfall. Santa Fe has an average of about 14 inches of rain a year.

Think and Apply

❶ What is the average rainfall in Phoenix, Arizona?

❷ Which city has the lowest average rainfall?

❸ Look at the cities in the Southwest region—Santa Fe and Phoenix. How is the rainfall in these cities different from the rainfall in Buffalo and Mobile?

History of the Navajo

Long ago the Navajo moved from place to place. They hunted and gathered food as they moved. Some historians think that the Navajo originally came to the Southwest from Canada.

The Navajo met a group called the Pueblo (PWEB loh) when they arrived in the area now known as the Four Corners. The Pueblo had lived in this area long before the Navajo arrived. The Pueblo were skilled farmers and builders.

The Navajo liked the Pueblo way of life. They decided to settle near the Pueblo. The Navajo learned how to grow corn, melons, and squash from the Pueblo.

In the 1600s Spanish settlers brought sheep to the Southwest. The Navajo became expert shepherds, raising large flocks of sheep. The Navajo also received horses, cattle, and goats from the Spanish.

▲ The Navajo are skilled at raising sheep.

▼ About 8,000 Navajo were forced to go on the Long Walk. Many of the Navajo died.

Over time American settlers began moving to the Southwest. They built farms on Navajo land. Sometimes the settlers and the Navajo did not get along.

In 1864 the United States Army sided with the settlers. Soldiers forced the Navajo to move from Arizona to New Mexico. This trip was called the Long Walk. It was more than 300 miles long. Many Navajo died along the way. In 1868 the United States government decided to allow the Navajo to return home.

▲ This Navajo family lives in Utah.

Today the Navajo are one of the largest Native American groups in the United States. The Navajo Reservation has its own school system and newspapers. It is the largest reservation in the United States.

REVIEW How did meeting the Pueblo help to change the Navajo way of life?
Main Idea and Details

FACT FILE

Speaking Secrets

During World War II, many Navajo served in the United States armed forces. Some Navajo soldiers helped send top-secret messages. These soldiers were called Code Talkers. They helped the military create a secret code based on the Navajo language. The Navajo language is hard to learn. It is not similar to any languages spoken in Europe or Asia. Only Navajo Code Talkers could understand the code. The Code Talkers used radios to send messages about battle plans. Enemy soldiers could not understand the coded messages. These Navajo soldiers helped the United States and its allies win World War II.

Government of the Navajo

Long ago the Navajo lived in many small bands. These bands, or groups of families, built their hogans many miles away from other bands. Each band governed itself.

The people in each band also belonged to a clan. You learned about clans when studying the Iroquois. A clan is a group of people who are all related. Today there are about 70 to 80 different Navajo clans.

Today the Navajo Nation's system of government is much like the United States government. The Navajo Nation has a president, lawmakers, and other leaders.

▲ The Navajo flag

▼ In the Navajo Nation Council Chamber, laws that affect the Navajo Reservation are discussed.

Within the Navajo Nation, the reservation is divided into smaller areas called chapters. Each chapter elects its own local leaders. These leaders run schools and organize local festivals.

Other leaders are elected to serve on the Navajo Nation Council. The council creates laws that affect the entire Navajo Nation. The council government meets four times a year in Window Rock.

REVIEW Describe the government of the Navajo Nation. **Summarize**

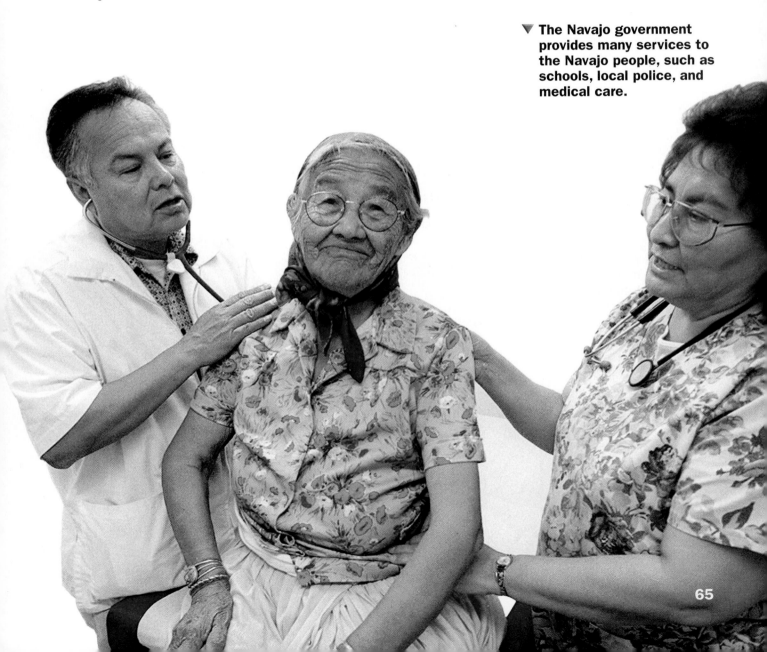

▼ The Navajo government provides many services to the Navajo people, such as schools, local police, and medical care.

Economy of the Navajo

Since the 1600s, the Navajo have raised goats, cattle, sheep, and horses. Men used the horses for hunting and to help them keep

▲ A young Navajo girl watches her family's sheep.

track of sheep. Young boys and older men looked after the sheep. Sheep were the most important livestock. Many Navajo still herd sheep today.

The Navajo depended on sheep for mutton and wool. They ate mutton, which is the meat from adult sheep. The Navajo fed mutton to visitors to welcome them.

The Navajo wove sheep's wool into blankets and rugs. In the spring, Navajo men cut off the sheep's wool. The women washed, spun, and dyed the wool. Young girls helped their mothers weave the wool. Beautiful, traditional designs were woven into the rugs and blankets. The Navajo people still are known for their weaving.

▶ A Navajo woman shows her daughter how to weave a traditional blanket.

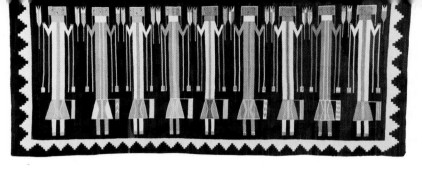

The Navajo often traded these rugs and blankets with other Native American groups. The Navajo still sell their rugs and blankets to the public. These rugs and blankets are often seen as works of art and are highly prized.

Today the Navajo work at many different jobs. Some have jobs with companies that mine coal or other minerals, such as copper, silver, and zinc. Others work for companies that produce electricity. Still others are doctors, lawyers, teachers, and other professionals. The Navajo Nation runs businesses, such as shopping centers, where many people work.

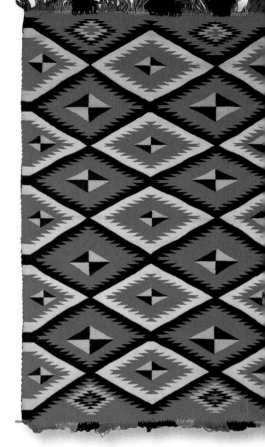

▲ Two Navajo rugs (top left and above) show different traditional designs.

REVIEW What resources play a part in the Navajo economy? **Draw Conclusions**

▼ Navajo today have many different jobs, including park ranger and teacher.

Culture of the Navajo

The Navajo share many customs and beliefs. Long ago the many Navajo bands gathered to take part in ceremonies for births, marriages, and deaths. These ceremonies taught the separate bands about the Navajo way of life. Many of these ceremonies still take place in the Navajo community.

Corn has been an important crop since the Navajo began farming. It is used in Navajo ceremonies also. When Navajo children were born, their parents sprinkled their faces with corn dust. The dust was a symbol of good luck.

Navajo women often go through a traditional ceremony when they marry. As part of the ceremony, they grind corn for three days. After they finish they help make a cornmeal cake for the whole community.

A traditional religious ceremony that is still used today is sandpainting. The Navajo mix crushed, colored sandstone with charcoal, pollen, and corn dust. This special sand is made in white, blue, yellow, black, and red. The Navajo make large pictures called sand paintings by pouring the colored sand onto a background of smooth, plain sand. The paintings are of important Navajo religious symbols. They are used in ceremonies, especially when people are sick.

▲ A Navajo sand painting

▼ These Navajo girls are grinding corn for a coming-of-age ceremony.

All Navajo groups have special songs, called chants, for important events. These chants are still a part of the community today. Special people, called chanters, perform these chants. People sing these chants for sick people and for soldiers returning from war. Chants are also used to bless a new home or school or a couple when they marry.

The Navajo share their culture through festivals, such as the Navajo Nation Fair in Window Rock. Visitors eat traditional Navajo foods, such as mutton stew or corn soup. Visitors also listen to Navajo music. They watch artists and craftspeople make rugs and other crafts. The Navajo have held this fair every summer for almost 60 years. It is the largest Native American fair in the United States.

REVIEW Describe some ways that the Navajo have used corn in their ceremonies. **Summarize**

▼ Dancers prepare for competition at the Navajo Nation Fair.

1. Describe the climate and land-forms of the Southwest region.

2. What was the Long Walk?

3. How is the government of the Navajo Nation like the government of the United States?

4. What did the men do to help make blankets and rugs? What did the women and young girls do?

5. Why are sheep an important part of the Navajo economy?

6. **Use a Bar Graph** Make a bar graph that shows the number of students in four different classrooms in your school, including your own. Put the number of students along the side of the graph. Put the room number or the teachers' names at the bottom.

Link to ⦵⦵ Writing

Write a Brochure: **Write one or two paragraphs describing what a visitor to the Navajo Nation Fair could expect to see and do.**

Test Talk

Use Information from Graphics

Directions: Think about where you need to look for an answer. Follow these steps.

- Read the question.
- Look for and circle key words in the question.
- Use details from the image or graphic to answer the question.

1. Look at the photograph below. Use information from the photograph to answer the question. How can you tell that this is a dry environment? Use details to support your answer.

   To find the answer, I will look at the photograph and tell what it shows.

   My Answer: The land in the photograph has very few trees or grass and looks like a desert.

   Try it Look at the photograph at left. Use information from the photograph to answer the question. Write your answer on a separate sheet of paper.

2. What is the man on horseback doing? Use details to support your answer.

   To find the answer, I will_____

   My Answer: _____

These projects will help you learn about other Native American groups.

People of the Southwest

Make a Fact Card. Choose a Native American group from the Southwest, such as the Navajo, Hopi, Apache, or Pueblo. Research the different clothing, crops, and building materials used by the people in that group. Create a fact card. On the front of the card, write the name of your group. On the back of the card, write five interesting facts about the group. Now trade cards with your classmates to learn about many different groups.

Hopi

1. The Hopi grew 24 different types of corn.
2. The Hopi lived in pueblos made of mud and stone.
3.
4.
5.

Landforms of the Southwest

Draw a Picture. Landforms are special shapes on Earth's surface. Mountains and valleys are examples of landforms. Native Americans in the Southwest lived among many beautiful landforms. In a dictionary or encyclopedia, look up these landforms: butte, canyon, mesa, plateau. Write a definition of each landform. Then draw a picture of each one.

The Haida

The Haida used canoes such as this one to fish and travel along the water.

Hello, my name is Annie. I am a member of the Haida (HEYE duh) Nation. Haida means "people" in my language. I live with my family in Hydaburg, Alaska. Our town is on Prince of Wales Island. Our island is in southeast Alaska. There are many islands in the area.

The Haida are one of many Native American groups who live on the Northwest Coast. This region stretches from northern California through Canada and Alaska.

The climate on most of the Northwest Coast is mild and wet. An ocean current runs along the coast. A **current** is a flow of water in the ocean. As this current flows through the ocean, it warms the ocean and the air above it. Many parts of the region get heavy rainfall because of mountains and winds.

The Northwest Coast has many natural resources. The ocean and rivers are filled with fish and shellfish. For hundreds of years, the Haida have fished and also hunted for seals, sea lions, and sea otters in the waters surrounding the islands.

Forests of cedar trees still cover the islands where the Haida live. Long ago my ancestors made almost everything they needed from cedar trees. They wove clothes, ropes, baskets, and mats from the cedar bark. They hollowed-out cedar logs to make dugouts, which are a type of canoe. They also built houses from cedar planks, or thick boards.

Keep reading to learn more about the Haida.

▲ **Decorations on Haida houses told about the families who lived there.**

REVIEW Why were cedar forests important to the Haida? **Summarize**

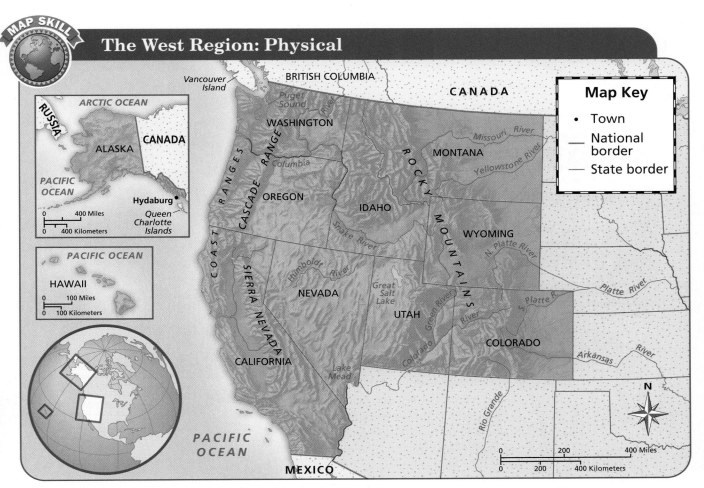

The West Region: Physical

MAP SKILL

Map Key
- Town
— National border
— State border

▲ **The Haida live along the Northwest Coast of North America.**

MAP SKILL Understand Inset Maps *Why are Hawaii and Alaska shown on inset maps?*

Internet Search Engine

What? The Internet is a useful tool for finding information about almost any topic. One of the fastest and easiest ways to find information about a topic on the Internet is to use a search engine. A **search engine** is a special Web site that looks for other Web sites on the World Wide Web. It looks for Web sites that have information on the topic you are researching.

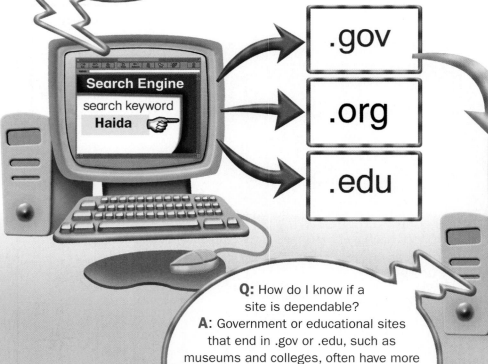

Q: How do I begin my search?
A: Start with a search engine. Then type in a keyword or keywords for the information you want.

Search Engine
search keyword
Haida

.gov

.org

.edu

The Haida

Q: How do I know if a site is dependable?
A: Government or educational sites that end in .gov or .edu, such as museums and colleges, often have more dependable information than other sites. Also, use what you have learned about telling fact from opinion to judge how dependable a Web site is.

Why? The World Wide Web has so much information that it would be almost impossible to find what you need without help. A search engine gives you that help. You type in a few words about your subject, and the search engine quickly searches the Internet for Web sites related to your subject. Search engines check millions of Web sites in a very short time. Search engines make it much easier to use the Internet for research.

How? To use a search engine, follow these steps.

1. Select a search engine. A teacher or librarian can help you choose a good search engine.

2. Type in a keyword or two. A **keyword** is a word that has to do with what you are researching, such as "Haida." Then click on "Search." You may have to try different words. If you need help, click on "Help" or "Search Tips."

3. If your search brings no results, try another keyword, or ask for help from someone who uses the Internet.

4. If your search gives you too many results, you can add more search words. For example, after "Haida" you could type "food" or "culture."

5. Check the facts you find on the Internet with another source.

Think and Apply

❶ What is one way an Internet **search engine** can be a useful research tool?

❷ What **keywords** would you use to begin a search on Native Americans of the Northwest Coast?

❸ What keywords would you use to find a map of Hydaburg, where Annie lives?

History of the Haida

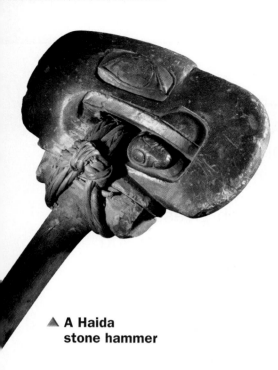

▲ A Haida
stone hammer

At one time most Haida lived on the Queen Charlotte Islands near the coast of Canada. They called their islands Haida Gwaii (ka WY). *Haida Gwaii* means "Land of the People." They built their villages along the shores of the islands.

The Haida used dugout canoes to travel back and forth to the mainland. They hunted and gathered food on the mainland. The Haida learned how to make knives and other stone tools from other groups in the area. They used these tools to hunt and prepare food.

As the Haida population grew, Haida Gwaii became too crowded. A group of Haida moved to southeastern Alaska about 300 years ago.

▼ Because the Haida depended on the sea, their homes were usually built close to the shore.

The Haida called this new settlement Kaigani (KI gone NE) Haida. Many scholars believe that another reason for the move was to be closer to important trade routes.

Settlers in Kaigani Haida were very successful. They traded with Russian traders and other Native Americans. They soon became the largest Native American group in the area.

Annie and her family members are descendants of the people who moved to Kaigani Haida long ago. So are many of those who live in Hydaburg today. Haida also still live in the Queen Charlotte Islands.

REVIEW Why did many Haida leave Haida Gwaii? **Cause and Effect**

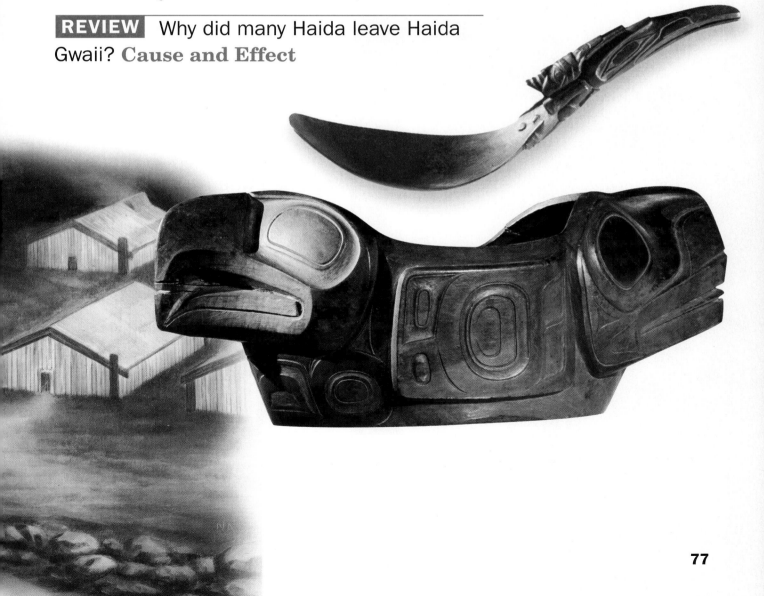

▼ Skillfully carved objects like this wooden dish and wooden spoon could be used or traded.

Government of the Haida

In the past each Haida village was made up of several large houses. Closely related families lived together in the same house. Often 30 or 40 people lived in one Haida house, with as many as 100 people in the largest houses.

Each house had its own chief. The chief represented his house in community decisions. The chief of the largest house with the most belongings was also the chief of the village. The village chief usually built his house in the center of the village.

The village chief made many important decisions, but he did not act alone. He worked with other village leaders and people from his house. Together, they decided when and where to fish. They decided where to build new houses and hold celebrations.

▼ This is the house of a Haida chief from Queen Charlotte Island. The Haida dug deep into the earth to make their homes larger and more comfortable.

▲ Haida leaders wear traditional clothing at a ceremony celebrating a new canoe.

◀ Birds and animals are important symbols used to represent people, ideas, and clans. An eagle is pictured here. It is an important clan symbol.

Wealth was very important to the Haida of the past. Wealth to the Haida meant having the most possessions and food supplies. The more a family had, the more influential the family was in community decisions. People's jobs, and even the way they were buried when they died, depended on how much wealth they had. But giving things away was also important. People were respected both for what they had and for what they gave away.

Today Haida villages have Village Councils that make important decisions for each village. Many Haida are also part of the Council of the Haida Nation. The Council works to protect Haida land rights.

The Haida also belong to the North Coast Tribal Council. The North Coast Tribal Council brings together groups from Canada and Alaska. Council members work together on issues that affect Native Americans.

Central Council
Tlingit and Haida
Indian Tribes of Alaska

▲ The Tlingit and Haida are closely related. In addition to their own local governments, they share a combined council that handles issues related to their region.

REVIEW How were important decisions made in Haida villages? Summarize

Economy of the Haida

▲ A Haida father and son check the traps they will use to catch crabs.

In the past the Haida depended on the sea for most of their food. Fish were the most important part of their diet. They ate salmon and halibut. They also ate sea animals, such as seals and sea otters, and gathered shellfish.

Haida boys learned how to fish, hunt, and build houses and canoes at an early age. Their fathers taught them wood carving and painting. Girls gathered wild plants and shellfish for food. They helped the women in the house cook. The girls also looked after younger children and made clothing and baskets.

Every summer the Haida caught thousands of salmon during the time called the salmon run. The salmon run is when salmon leave the ocean and swim into the rivers to lay eggs. During these months, millions of salmon swim up the rivers.

The men caught salmon in traps or cedar-bark nets, or used spears to catch them. Haida women dried and salted the fish to make them last longer. These fish provided food all year long.

The Haida traded with other Native American groups such as the Tlingit (KLINHNG it) and Tsimshian (chim SHE an). The Haida traded canoes, wooden objects, and baskets for copper, clothing, and candlefish. Candlefish are a type of fish. The Haida also traded with Europeans for goods such as metal tools and blankets.

▼ The Haida hunted seals for food and for their skins. Seal skins were stretched on frames like this one and dried in the sun.

Today the Haida have many different jobs. Some Haida own fishing companies. Other Haida own businesses that offer many different services, such as providing tours of the islands to visitors or repairing computers.

▼ Carved wooden Haida boxes were valuable trade goods.

REVIEW Why was the salmon run important to the Haida? **Main Idea and Details**

▲ Haida in a canoe travel with fishing boats on a ceremonial trip.

FACT FILE

Bright Fish

The Haida traded with groups like the Tlingit for small fish called *eulachon* [YOO lah kon], or candlefish. They ate the fish and used its oil to add flavor to their food. They also dried the fish and put strings through them. The dried fish burned just like a candle when the string was lit. The oil in the candlefish made the flame burn brightly and steadily.

During some ceremonies, a very rich host family would pour large amounts of candlefish oil into the fire. This made a huge flame. The host family impressed guests with their wealth by pouring the valuable oil onto the fire.

Culture of the Haida

The Haida did not have to hunt on the land much of the year. The sea and the rivers provided most of their food. This gave them time for many other activities. Haida craftspeople decorated beautiful boxes and wove blankets. The Haida were especially skilled wood carvers. They carved canoes, chests, and masks.

Today Haida wood carvers still make large wooden carvings called totem poles. The figures on a totem pole might tell a story about the families in a house. Other totem poles remember important people. Often artists carve birds and animals on the totem poles. Visitors to Totem Park in Hydaburg can see totem poles made by early Haida.

The Haida still hold many dances, feasts, and ceremonies. One very important ceremony for the Haida and other groups in the Northwest Coast is the potlatch. A **potlatch** is a time of gift giving and sharing food. A family has a potlatch when they celebrate a special event, such as a wedding, graduation, or birth. Some guests travel hundreds of miles to attend a potlatch.

▲ Many totem poles from old villages have been restored.

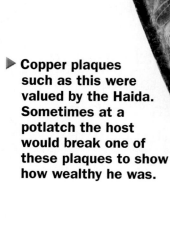

▶ Copper plaques such as this were valued by the Haida. Sometimes at a potlatch the host would break one of these plaques to show how wealthy he was.

At potlatches, people trade news and tell stories. They eat, sing, play games, and dance. The stories at the potlatch help the Haida remember their history.

The family that holds the potlatch gives gifts to all the guests. Potlatches allow families to share their belongings and good fortune. Today potlatch gifts may include money and household goods. In the past some guests might receive otter skins, dried fish, or carved wooden boxes. The most important guests might be given a robe decorated with shells and animal teeth, or even a canoe. Some families spent many years collecting gifts for their potlatch. A family gained respect in the community by giving many gifts.

REVIEW What happens during a Haida potlatch? **Summarize**

▲ Many Northwest Coast artists still make beautiful wood carvings.

▼ A potlatch in Metlakatla, Alaska

Review

1. How do ocean currents affect the climate on the Northwest Coast?

2. Why were rivers and the ocean important to the Haida way of life?

3. How did contact with European traders affect Haida villagers?

4. What made the village chief different from other village leaders?

5. How did the Haida in the past catch fish during the salmon run?

6. Why do the Haida hold potlatches?

7. **Use an Internet Search Engine**
Suppose you are writing a report on another Northwest Coast Native American group, such as the Tlingit or the Tsimshian. What keywords could you use in an Internet search engine to find information about that group?

Link to 〜 Writing

Write a Field Report: Suppose you are a trader who is staying in a Haida village. Write a report for people back home describing the appearance of the village and the types of jobs done by men and women.

Test Talk

Strategy 6: Write Your Answer to Score High

Directions: If you are asked to write an answer to a question, here are some simple steps to follow. These steps will help you make sure your answer is correct, complete, and focused.

- Read the question.
- Make notes about details that answer the question.
- Reread the question and your notes. Add details if needed.
- Use details from your notes to answer the question.
- Check your answer. Ask yourself:
  Is my answer correct?
  Is my answer complete?
  Is my answer focused? Do all my details help answer the question?

Examine this example by a student named Marco. What should he do to score higher?

1. What were some reasons that cedar trees were important to the Haida?

   Marco's notes: They made houses from cedar wood.

   Marco's answer: Cedar trees were important because the Haida used them to build houses.

To score higher, Marco needs to add more reasons why cedar trees were important. Marco circled key words in the question. Marco's notes are not complete. Can you write a better answer?

Try It 2. Examine this example. A student named Clara completed it. What should she do to score higher?

   What sources of food did the Haida depend on?

   Clara's notes: Salmon

   Clara's answer: One Haida food source was salmon.

To score higher, Clara needs to_____

_____

These projects will help you learn about other Native American groups.

Canoe Builders

Make a model. The Haida were famous for the large and beautiful canoes they built. They used these canoes for fishing, traveling, and attacking their enemies. Most canoes had designs on the front that told a story about the owner. Other groups, such as the Iroquois and the Creek, also made canoes. Pick a Native American group from the Northwest and use the Internet and other sources to find out what their canoes looked like. Make a small model of a canoe to show the class.

People of the Northwest Coast

Create a mural. At one time, more than 80 different Native American groups lived along the Northwest Coast. They spoke many different languages. Each group had its own customs and traditions. Choose several groups, such as the Bella Coola (bell LA coo LA), Tillamook (till LA mak), Tlingit, or Haida, and work with classmates to create a mural. The mural should show how different groups dressed, celebrated festivals, and obtained food.

Index

Titles appear in italics. An *m* in front of a page number indicates a map.
A *p* in front of a page number indicates a picture.

Credits

MAPS
Mapquest.com, Inc.

ILLUSTRATIONS
4 Neal Armstrong
19 Susan J. Carlson
33, 62, 76 Andy Zito;
36 Tony Crnkovich
40 Darch Clampitt

PHOTOGRAPHS
Every effort has been made to secure permission and provide appropriate credit for photographic material. The publisher deeply regrets any omission and pledges to correct errors called to its attention in subsequent editions.

Unless otherwise acknowledged, all photographs are the property of Scott Foresman, a division of Pearson Education.

Photo locators denoted as follows: Top (T), Center (C), Bottom (B), Left (L), Right (R), Background (Bkgd)

Cover
(BR) ©Reinhard Brucker/Westwind Enterprises
(C) ©2004 Clark James Mishler/AlaskaStock.com
(TR) ©Ric Ergenbright/Corbis
(Bkgd) ©Lowe Art Museum/SuperStock
(TL) ©Bridgeman Art Library, London/SuperStock
(TCL) ©Werner Forman/Art Resource, NY
(TC) ©Marilyn "Angel" Wynn/nativestock.com
(TCR) Van Zelst Family Collection

Front Matter
vii (L) ©Nativestock, (C) ©Carnegie Museum of Natural History, (R) Reinhard Brucker/Westwind Enterprises

Unit 1
2 (T) Werner Forman/Art Resource, NY, (BL) digitalvisiononline.com, (B) SuperStock, (BR) ©Galen Rowell/Corbis
3 Getty Images
4 Runk/ Schoenberger/Grant Heilman Photography
5 Moundville Archaeological Park, The University of Alabama
6 (T) ©Michelle Garrett/Corbis
7 (B) Marilyn "Angel" Wynn/Nativestock, (BC) Reinhard Brucker/Westwind Enterprises
9 ©George Gerster/Photo Researchers, Inc.
10 (T) ©Werner Forman/Art Resource, NY, (B) ©Raymond Gehman/Corbis
11 (T) ©Werner Forman/Art Resource, NY, (B) Moundville Archaeological Park, The University of Alabama
13 ©Richard A. Cooke/ Corbis

Unit 2
16 Marilyn "Angel" Wynn/Nativestock
18 The Granger Collection, New York
20 ©J. A. Kraulis/Masterfile Corporation
22 (T) Carnegie Museum of Natural History, (BL) Corbis, (BR) AP/Wide World Photos
24 Marilyn "Angel" Wynn/Nativestock
25 (T) Westwind Enterprises, (B) ©Mike Greenlar/The Image Works, Inc.
26 (T) Marilyn "Angel" Wynn/Nativestock, (B) ©Lawrence Migdale/www.migdale.com
27 (TR) ©Reinhard Brucker/Westwind Enterprises, (B) Corbis

Unit 3
30 (BL) ©Marilyn "Angel" Wynn/Nativestock, (BR) SuperStock, (T) Nativestock
32 Marilyn "Angel" Wynn/Nativestock
34 Getty Images
36 Muscogee Nation News
37 AP/Wide World Photos
38 ©Marilyn "Angel" Wynn/Nativestock
39 Muscogee Nation News
41 Kit H. Breen;

Unit 4
44 (TL) Nativestock, (B) ©Nik Wheeler/Corbis
45 (T) ©Tom Bean/Getty Images
46 (T) Westwind Enterprises
47 (T) ©National Archives, Washington DC/Art Resource, NY, (B) ©Dewall/Corbis/Sygma
48 ©Smithsonian American Art Museum, Washington, DC/Art Resource, NY
49 (B) ©Robert Van Der Hilst/Corbis
50 (B) ©Buffalo Bill Historical Center Cody Wyoming / Mireille Vautier/The Art Archive, (T) ©Werner Forman/Art Resource, NY
51 (T) Getty Images, (B) ©Myrleen Ferguson Cate/PhotoEdit
52 (T) ©Chuck Schmeiser/Unicorn Stock Photos, (B) ©Werner Forman/Art Resource, NY
53 (T) ©Kent & Donna Dannen, (B) ©AFP/Getty Images
55 (B) R Dewall/Corbis, ©John Coletti/Folio Inc.

Unit 5
58 (T) ©Donald C. & Priscilla Alexander Eastman/Lonely Planet Images, (B) ©Joe Sohm/The Image Works, Inc.
59 ©Don Getsug/Photo Researchers, Inc.
60 ©James Randklev/ Stone
61 ©Danny Daniels/Index Stock Imagery;
62 (T) ©Kevin Fleming/ Corbis
63 (B) Corbis, (T) ©Robert Huntzinger/Corbis
65 AP/Wide World Photos
66 (T) ©Branson Reynolds/Index Stock Imagery, (B) ©Paul Chesley/Getty Images
67 (TL, TR) Christie's Images/Corbis, (BR) ©Kevin Fleming /Corbis, (BL) ©S. Grandadam/Robert Harding Picture Library/Alamy Images
68 (T) ©G.L. French/Robertstock.com, (B) ©John Running
69 ©Masha Nordbye/Bruce Coleman Inc.
70 ©Mary Rhodes/Animals Animals

Unit 6
72 (T, B) Alaska Stock, (B) Marilyn "Angel" Wynn/Nativestock
73 (T) ©Emily Riddell/Lonely Planet Images
76 (T) ©Werner Forman/Art Resource, NY
77 (B) ©Werner Forman/Art Resource, NY
78 (L) ©Canadian Museum of Civilization/Corbis, (R) ©Dewitt Jones/Corbis
79 (T) ©Werner Forman/Art Resource, NY, (B) ©Courtesy of Central Council Tlingit & Haida Indian Tribes of Alaska
80 (T) ©Frank Straub/Index Stock Imagery, (B) ©Dewitt Jones/Corbis
81 (T) Canadian Museum of Civilization/Corbis, (B) Alaska Stock
82 (T) ©Tom Bean/Corbis, (B) ©Werner Forman/Art Resource, NY
83 (B) ©Lawrence Migdale/www.migdale.com, (T) AP/Wide World Photos